KU-191-748

The Fabian Society

The Fabian Society has played a central role for more than a century in the development of political ideas and public policy on the left of centre. Analysing the key challenges facing the UK and the rest of the industrialised world in a changing society and global economy, the Society's programme aims to explore the political ideas and the policy reforms which will define progressive politics in the new century.

The Society is unique among think tanks in being a democratically-constituted membership organisation. It is affiliated to the Labour Party but is editorially and organisationally independent. Through its publications, seminars and conferences, the Society provides an arena for open-minded public debate.

Fabian Society
11 Dartmouth Street
London SW1H 9BN
www.fabian-society.org.uk

Fabian ideas
Series editor: Ellie Levenson

First published March 2003

ISBN 0 7163 0606 9
ISSN 1469 0136

This book, like all publications of the Fabian Society, represents not the collective views of the Society but only the views of the author. This publication may not be reproduced without express permission of the Fabian Society.

British Library Cataloguing in Publication data.
A catalogue record for this book is available from the British Library.

Printed by Bell & Bain Limited, Glasgow

Contents

About the authors

Colin Crouch is Professor of Sociology at the European University Institute, Florence, and External Scientific member of the Max Planck Institute for Society Reserach, Cologne. He is Chair of the editorial board of the *Political Quarterly*, of which he was previously joint editor. He was Chair of the Fabian Society in 1976. His recent books include *Industrial Relations and European State Traditions* (1993), *Are Skills the Answer?* (with David Finegold and Mari Sako, 1999), *Social Change in Western Europe* (1999) and *Coping with Post-democracy* (2000). *Coping with Post-democracy* won the Jenny Jeger prize for best Fabian Society Publication in 2001.

1 | The clash between citizenship and commercialisation

Since 1997 the Labour Government has made clear that its highest priority in domestic policy is the improvement of public services. It starts from the premise that public services – notably in education and health – are in general underperforming. The centrepiece of its programme for reform has been and is the use of the private sector to provide various kinds of public services. The use of private provision was introduced by previous Conservative Governments, but has been extended in important ways by New Labour.

Argument over the role of private firms in the provision of public services has mainly been waged in terms of efficiency. Is the Government right that, because they have been tried and tested in the competitive market, private businesses will generally provide a superior and more cost-effective service than public organisations? Do the Private Finance Initiative (PFI) and other forms of Public-Private Partnerships (PPP) give better value for money than their purely public equivalents? A number of studies have examined the evidence on these questions, most of them in fact concluding that use of the private sector does not lead to greater efficiency.[1]

Governments and their advisers believe that private firms will necessarily bring increased efficiency to public services, because they have been tested in the market; an inefficient private firm disappears under the impact of competitive pressure, so the survivors are known to be efficient. There is no similar mechanism in public service, it is argued. If the private firms are small and selling successfully in an almost perfect market to ultimate consumers, the argument is a strong one. However, as we move away from these conditions towards those more typical of much of the area of contracted-out public services, its power weakens.

First, the primary duty of a private firm is to maximise shareholder value. This coincides with meeting customers' needs efficiently in a near-perfect market, because a firm which ignores this need will lose business. However, where competition is imperfect or where contracts can be won by insider lobbying rather than by demonstrating superior performance, the link between shareholders' profits and efficiency for the customer is weakened. This is frequently the case with public-service contracts, as shown at several points below.

Second, the superior efficiency argument depends heavily on the dogmatic assumption that abstract general management skills are more important than those specific to the activity concerned. Since the specific knowledge relevant to most public services is a virtual monopoly of the public sector, firms bidding for these contracts usually come from other parts of the economy. For example, when a road construction company enters the business of running primary schools, it has to be believed that the gain that comes from its knowledge of general management outweighs the inefficiency loss that flows from its inexperience of education.

Third, most of the managers and other staff who work in a private firm do not themselves have a direct stake in the firm's profits. Analogues of this stake are constructed for them by top management to give them incentives to maximise performance. Their own motivation is similar to that of persons working in a public service organisation; they respond to the incentive structure established by top management. If the top political level is itself committed to maximising efficiency, it is able to use techniques derived from the private sector to convert this motive into incentives for middle management, as the Conservative Governments of the 1980s did in several areas. It is not necessary to use private contractors themselves to achieve this.

Fourth, and as will again be discussed in more detail below, many of the techniques important to private service managers in achieving efficiency are not available in the public service. For example, an important skill of private management lies in identifying the firm's target market, who does it want to be its customers? This skill cannot be transferred to a national education system unless it is considered acceptable that some children should be offered no school at all.

Finally, also addressed in detail below, in public service contracts efficiency for the customer does not necessarily coincide with satisfaction for the ultimate consumer. The customer is a government department, not the actual user of a service, and it is possible to imagine many situations where the interests of government and citizens are not identical.

These last two points take us beyond a simple value for money approach to efficiency, and raise the question of efficiency for whom? This brings us to the central issue that I want to address in this pamphlet: how does use of the private sector to deliver public services affect, not the efficiency, but the very character of such services?

Post-industrial capitalism

Attempts at marrying what have until now been primarily public services with capitalist practices take a variety of forms: markets within public ownership; privatisation with or without fully free markets; contracting out both capital projects and service delivery, sometimes without either privatisation or markets. The relationship of the market to private ownership is more ambiguous than is often assumed. Certainly perfect markets alongside private ownership of economic resources provide the conditions for the capitalism of economics text-books, and the two criteria fit together well. It is however entirely possible to have markets without private ownership: an authority owning collective resources can decide to use a system of prices to make a market through which to allocate these resources within a public or charitable service. This idea informed many Conservative reforms of the 1980s. Government departments and service units were required to trade services with other units as though they were in a market relationship, abandoning the professional colleague model that had previously governed their interactions. A major example was the internal market introduced into the National Health Service. It has largely fallen to New Labour to take the further step of introducing private profit-making firms into what had been, under the Conservatives, still public service – though often this paradoxically takes the form of private provision without true markets.

The generic term which will be used here for all these practices is commercialisation, because each is premised on the assumption that the quality of public services will be improved if the existing practices and ethos of public service are replaced by those typical of commercial practice. This concept is more accurate than that of marketisation, for some of the processes now being introduced involve distortions of the market rather than its purification. And it is more general than privatisation, which strictly speaking refers only to the transfer of ownership of assets.

Although capitalism originated in post-mediæval Europe in services sectors which have again become fundamental to it – mainly banking – it fully took wing with industrialisation. The greatly enlarged production of material goods which this made possible released the spiral of investment in plant and equipment, production and sale of a good, and further investment of the proceeds from these sales which became the great engine of 19th and 20th century wealth and prosperity. But capitalism expands its scope, not just by developing new goods and production methods, but also by pulling more and more areas of life within the spiral. Services which might have been rendered as, say, a community or family obligation are transformed into wage labour and sold. Much of the political conflict of the last two centuries concerned the boundaries which a great diversity of other interests – for example, churches and the working class – sought to erect around this rampaging force.[2]

Various compromises were eventually established. Sundays and other religious holidays were more or less protected from the grasp of the working week; family life remained uncommodified, mainly through the withdrawal of the majority of married women from the labour market; various limits were imposed on the exploitation of labour; and by the mid-20th century a series of basic services were at least partly removed from the reach of capitalism, because their provision was considered too important. As T H Marshall memorably argued, people acquired rights to these goods and services, mainly the latter, by virtue of their status as citizens, and not because they were able to buy them in the market.[3] Just as it became a mark of democracy that the right to vote or to a fair trial were not available for market purchase, so with entitlement to certain services; provision of them through market means would demean their citizenship quality. They were not necessarily delivered free of charge, but any charges were notional, and designed explicitly not to be used as rationing or allocation devices.

The list of items included in what we can call 'citizenship services' has varied across societies and over time, but usually

5

includes entitlement to certain levels of education, health services, certain forms of care service in case of need, financial support in old age and in the event of temporary or permanent loss of earning capacity through unemployment, ill health or injury.

Although conflicts over these exclusions from the reach of the market were often intense, the task of those trying to achieve them was made easier by the fact that for most of the period the best opportunities for profit and extending the scope of the market lay in industrial production. This was particularly true in the years around the Second World War, when the exigencies of increasingly technological warfare stimulated invention, research and development in many fields, with manifold subsequent peacetime uses. Important compromises over labour rights and the welfare state were negotiated as western capitalism was relaxing into enjoying these possibilities. By the late 1960s and early 1970s this process had peaked. While innovations in the production of goods have continued apace, major new developments have required increasingly costly research and large-scale investment. At the same time many new opportunities began to open in the provision to an increasingly wealthy population of services rather than goods: new forms of distribution, increasing travel, new forms of financial and other business services, growing use of restaurants and other food outlets, more interest in taking advantage of health, education, legal and other professional services. Increasingly capitalist firms have sought their profits in these sectors as well as, and gradually instead of, manufacturing.

But this has raised a problem. Some services provided by the welfare state are potentially very profitable but are protected from private ownership and the market as part of the mid-century citizenship package. So long as the welfare state survives, potential areas of profit-making are excluded from capital's reach. Post-industrial capitalism has therefore started to try to undo the deals made by its industrial predecessor. It is now being aided in this by the World Trade Organisation (WTO), which has been charged by the governments of the world's most powerful countries with liberalising the international exchange of goods and services. It has no other responsibilities and recognises no other priorities. The only right it protects against open competition is the right of patent. In addition to liberalising existing markets, the WTO is now trying to introduce them into fields which have previously been governed by different principles. It has in particular identified the welfare state, including state education and health services, as areas which should be opened up to markets, or to privatisation.

But is opposition to this not just a knee-jerk reaction, based on outmoded prejudices? Markets and capitalist producers provide us reasonably efficiently with toothpaste, motor vehicles and banking facilities; why not let them do the same with schools and hospitals? That is what we must now investigate.

Citizenship and markets

An essential starting point for a critique of commercialisation is the observation that the maximisation of markets and private ownership can conflict with other social goals. While the WTO has not been given the mandate to consider these, individual governments, organisations and private persons are free to place markets into perspective and to debate whether they should be accepted uncritically as the sole criterion to govern our affairs. Almost no-one except a tiny number of extreme libertarians would disagree with this in principle. For example, virtually no-one believes that sexual relationships, or those between parents and children, should be forced into a market frame; or that national political sovereignty should be capable of being traded in the market; or that the ability of people to change their residence from country to country should be governed only by labour-market opportunities and not by state immigration policy.

The market is not capable of being an absolute principle, since it is a means for achieving ends and not an end in itself. The case for the market is that if we follow its rules we shall make allocation decisions that better reach our goals, whatever these are. Other means of making allocations always remain open to the doubt that they do not provide as efficient a means of calculating costs, including opportunity costs, as the actual market. But this does not dispose of two principal points: that the market can fail to register all relevant elements of a choice of good; and that its use can itself change negatively the quality of a good. The former criticism is of major practical importance, but it is at least capable of being remedied by improving the quality of the market itself, rather than by suppressing it. For example, if the price of a good fails to represent the costs of pollution created in its production, it is possible to impose a tax reflecting the cost of the pollution, which will then be reflected in the price.

The second objection, that use of the market per se negatively changes the sought good itself, is more fundamental. For example, most people consider that sexual relationships offered under conditions of prostitution are inherently inferior to non-marketed ones. Prostitution could doubtless be improved if its market were made more perfect; for example, if it were subject to no legal prohibitions, the level of exploitation it involved and its sordid conditions of service delivery would be alleviated. But that is not the main point of the objection, which relates to an absolute judgement of quality.

Can objections of this kind be considered to apply in the field of citizenship services? The issue turns on two principal problems that can be caused by the application of commercial principles: distortion and residualisation.

Distortion

Providing goods or services through markets involves an elaborate procedure of creating barriers of access so that we cannot get them without payment. Sometimes the character of a good itself has to be changed to do this. We accept these distortions or most goods and services would not be provided at all; most obviously, traders would not be willing to set up shops if we did not accept cash desks and the whole procedure of money exchange. There are instances however where the extent of distortion required so damages the quality of the good in question or erects barriers so artificial that one may reasonably doubt whether the gains from any efficiency improvement are worth the losses incurred: for example when entrepreneurs are allowed to fence off pieces of coastline and charge for access to beaches or cliff walks.

Another form of distortion occurs when artificial attempts are made to provide indicators that can serve as analogues of prices. Where markets are virtual and goods and services are not really traded, as with the NHS internal market, there is a strong temptation to use as an indicator those elements which can be easily measured, rather than the qualities of the good or service really at stake. Service providers are likely to concentrate on those aspects of their work which are included in the indicators, neglecting others, not because they are intrinsically less important but because they are less measurable. The Labour Government's attempts to benchmark reduction of certain waiting lists for medical treatment have produced several such distortions; health service managers and professionals concentrate resources on those items being assessed and made politically prominent by drawing off resources from other, less easily observed, parts of the service. The apparent efficiency gains of this kind of targeting can become quite illusory; if, as may well be the case, the easily measured items are not in fact the most important, there may even be a loss of real effectiveness. This can

9

be tackled by increasing the number of indicators, but that eventually leads to measurement overload and excessive complexity.

The value of an indicator depends on its ability to measure accurately the quality that the customer is seeking, and this can be in doubt, even in 'real' markets. Stock-exchange evaluations of companies often present biased and distorted estimates of a firm's long-term worth; the exchange rates of currencies often bear only a poor relationship to their respective purchasing power; relative incomes are not the only legitimate means of comparing the value of two occupations. The problem intensifies in the case of shadow or artificial markets, as in public service applications. Here the indicator is typically chosen by a political or administrative authority and not by users, with the result that it is likely to suit political or managerial criteria rather than the client sensitivity which is in principle a major objective of the exercise. In the stock-exchange-led form of capitalism that became dominant by the end of the 20th century, this problem of indicators ceased to be a matter of concern. As was seen with a large number of information technology firms, which had very high share values before they ever sold a product to a customer, the value of a firm's shares can become self-justifying: if enough people believe that the share value is an indicator of something important, they will buy the shares and the value will have justified itself. It is not acceptable for democratic welfare policy to develop in this way.

Degradation and residualisation

The market is often depicted as a realm of consumer sovereignty: firms can sell their goods and services only if we choose to buy them. But it is providers who initially choose their customers, by deciding on which segments of the market they wish to target their products. There can be no obligation on a firm to try to meet everyone's needs. Citizen services differ fundamentally from this in that they must be universally provided to the defined category of citizens. Where Public-Private Partnerships allow private providers to chose the segments they want, while the public service guarantees provision for those in whom the private sector has no interest, such provision becomes residual. We know both in theory and in practice from the works of scholars like Albert Hirschman[4] and Richard Titmuss,[5] that residual public services becomes services of poor quality, because only the poor and politically ineffective have to make use of them.

Matters become even worse when citizenship services are required to have residual status and degraded quality because government is deliberately making space for commercial provision. Such services are then excluded from the realms of both markets and citizenship. Public services of this kind cannot be described as 'citizenship': access to them is more a penalty than a right; and the essential citizenship mechanism of voice must not be made available to residual recipients or they might seek improvements that would break the rule of no competition with market provision. An important example may be taken from the world of employment placement and unemployment assistance. The logic of a neo-liberal market regime is to privatise as much employment placement as possible, leaving a public service to deal with the hard-to-place, the unemployed. They are then placed into a special, stigmatised form of employment service isolated from everyone else.

The current British debate, which does not envisage the use of market prices to ultimate consumers of education and health, limits the risk of residualisation, though as we shall see in the following chapter it does not entirely exclude it. But it fully envisages the use of pricing and markets in relation to intermediate customers and suppliers within the service provision chain, and we see how this can produce residualisation on a wide scale.

The degradation *of* markets

It has already been pointed out that there can be resort to private ownership or a contribution from private providers without marketisation of the service concerned, especially if by market we understand the pure market of the economics text-books. This requires a very large number (tending to infinity) of competing producers and customers, with low barriers to entry by new producers. The regulatory system must also confine itself to maintaining the conditions of perfect competition, and must offer absolutely no favours or privileges to individual producers or customers. These stringent conditions fulfil two purposes. First, they ensure the lowest possible prices consistent with keeping producers in the market. Under perfect competition every producer is a price taker; no-one is in a position to fix or even influence prices by their individual action. Second, the condition of anonymity that this condition and the requirement of no privileged access to the regulatory authority impose means that there can be no political interference to favour individual producers over others. Indeed, in neo-classical economics there is no scope for lobbying the regulatory authority on behalf of producer interests at all.

There are many goods and services where something like these conditions are fulfilled, but it is obviously not true of some others, where it is difficult to sustain large numbers of firms. Recent economic theory has compromised with the unrealistic nature of these conditions for oligopolistic sectors. It has been noted that very small numbers of giant firms can in fact compete very keenly indeed with each other on price; therefore oligopoly in sectors like petrol, and sheer monopoly in computer software, are not considered to offend against anti-trust regulations. However, this assumes that only price is of interest. It completely ignores the important political concerns about privileged lobbying of political authorities which the conditions of the pure market were also intended to address. For 18th century political economists, in particular Adam Smith, as well as such 20th century successors as Friedrich von Hayek, the guarantee of anonymity and the incapacity of any individual producer to affect the market alone were also important for political reasons, to avoid privileged insider lobbying.

This becomes of fundamental importance when we address privatisation and major exercises in public-service sub-contracting, for here lobbying and the development of special relationships with politicians and civil servants of the kind which very large, far from anonymous, firms can carry out, become acutely relevant. Securing the privatisation contract, establishing its terms, and planning its eventual renewal, have become occasions for intensive interaction between very small numbers of individuals representing corporations (often former ministers and civil servants), and current ministers and civil servants. Even if unwitting, there are clear risks to the maintenance of proper standards in public life in such exchanges. In the case of full privatisation, the fact that the firms involved are not perfect market agents is frequently recognised by the establishment of regulatory authorities to monitor the subsequent behaviour of the industry. There are then grounds for concern over the relationship between the regulator and the lobbyists. The claim made for privatisation that it would depoliticise an industry or service and prevent corruption was simply untrue.

A central part of the case for bringing private providers into public provision is that this will bring increased diversity. The market ensures diversity and innovation when a large number of firms is trying to find new ways to make a profit. Many of the ideas they produce fail, but some succeed, and new products and services appear. This works very well in markets where there is much scope for diversity and novelty, where there are many firms, and where there are no serious overall consequences if individual firms fail. Private 'markets' within the welfare state lack these characteristics. The number of producers is very small. The number of risks that can be taken with how schools and hospitals are run has to be low.

This does not mean that oligopolistic firms cannot provide diversity. Such firms are well equipped for making innovations provided their managers have a strong incentive to do so and can give further incentives to those lower down their hierarchies. Here private firms are in the same position as government organisations themselves, which can also, if they choose to do so, find incentives to encourage innovation among their staff despite the lack of competitive pressure. Outside pure markets there is little to distinguish oligopolies in the private sector from public bodies or charitable foundations.

Not only is the number of suppliers small, but so is the number of customers. Although the rhetoric of commercialisation invariably speaks of the users or clients of public services as 'customers', the term is falsely applied. A customer chooses a good or service in exchange for paying the demanded market price. The users of contracted-out public services are very rarely in this position: the customer is the government or other public authority which places the contract to provide the service. The ultimate user or consumer of the service may have little choice in the matter, and has no direct relationship with the provider, all of whose attention in winning custom is directed at representatives of the public authority concerned.

The market for public services is therefore one in which oligopolistic providers make deals with monopsonist customers. Most of the characteristics normally intended by the idea of the market are missing from such arrangements.

Privatising or contracting out?

The distinction between privatisation and contracting out requires further analysis. Under the former, ownership of a previously public resource is transferred to private firms. Under the latter, ownership remains with the public sector, but the performance of individual parts of the service is provided by profit-seeking firms, on contracts of varying length. There is clearly a difference. For example, in privatising the railways government could have retained ownership of the railway network and contracted out just the provision of train, station, and goods handling services – a solution it was forced to introduce following the failure of Railtrack in 2001.

This distinction is very important to the Labour Government, since its strategy towards health and education involves partnerships between public and private finance and sub-contracting service delivery, not privatisation. However, while these processes avoid loss of public ownership and of ultimate control of a public asset, they not only share but in fact intensify one of the most disturbing aspects of privatisation: privileged lobbying and access to ministers and civil servants – the monopsonist customers – by individual corporations. Precisely because there is no final transfer of assets in public private financial partnerships and contracting out, the relationship between public authority and private provider becomes a continuing one, and therefore the lobbying and temptations of mutual exchanges of favours becomes permanent. Both forms necessarily feature contracts of long duration. In the case of privately financed capital projects, like a hospital or large school, contracts have to be very long indeed, often over 30 years. Given the short lifespan of contemporary political and organisational arrangements, these are more than lifetime contracts. When only services are contracted out there is not the need for such very lengthy periods, but there are still certain sunk costs and also a lengthy learning curve for the private contractor. Contracts of five to seven years are normal.

During contracts of both these typical lengths, the principal becomes very dependent on the agent for the quality of delivery. There may be penalty clauses for non-delivery, but these and performance targets can be specified only for currently foreseen needs and objectives. Contracts are legally binding documents which cannot be easily amended to take account of change; long-term contracts are a curiously rigid and inflexible instrument to be adopting during a period which is normally seen as one requiring particularly rapid adaptability and flexibility.

In the case of the shorter-term service contracts, firms have to start thinking about contract renewal after a fairly short period. This certainly gives them incentives to perform well on the existing contract, but cultivating good relations with a decision-makers can also help.

It is particularly interesting to observe, as discussed in more detail in the next chapter, how a number of firms are emerging who are specialists in the general art of government contracting, and pursue contracts across a wide diversity of sectors – to take the real example of Serco, a firm that builds missile warning systems and inspects schools. Clearly such firms have no initial expertise and therefore no particular substantive value added to offer within a new field like education when they first enter it. Indeed, it is notable that they almost always recruit their profes-sional staff from the very public authorities – such as inspec-torates and local education authorities – to which they then contract back their services. What they possess rather is a specialist skill in winning and possibly managing government contracts from politicians and civil servants. This is not neces-sarily a skill which passes value added and service quality to the ultimate consumers. After all, the need for the skill could have been avoided simply by not bringing in the private agent at all.

Loss of the concept of public authority

Government's behaviour in relation to actual and potential private contractors, and uncritical acceptance of their participation in making the public policies from which they will benefit, draws attention to another loss involved in commercialisation: that of the meaning of public authority and public service itself. It is useful here to remember that public service was originally a Victorian, rather than a social democratic, concept. In other words, it was developed during the heyday of what we now often see as unrestrained capitalism. The explanation of the paradox is that, precisely because they were staking out the liberties of capitalism, and frequently encountering the points where these clashed with other values and interests, late 19th century reformers took seriously Adam Smith's concern that the business world could corrupt politics just as much as politics could corrupt business. Politicians and civil servants therefore needed an ethic of their own, which demanded from them conduct different from, though not hostile to, that of the business world. They frequently failed to live up to these ideals, which is why we often see the Victorian age as hypocritical, but the ideals were there. Public officials were expected to be very careful in their dealings with persons who represented concentrations of business power. They were also expected to maintain a sense of the public interest which was more than the sum of individual business ambitions. This idea developed out of the concept of the superior interests of the monarch, but it adapted itself to bourgeois life, and then reached its apogee in the social democratic ideal of the state as the servant of the universal citizen.

One of the changes introduced by 'new public management' during the 1980s was a redefinition of the boundary between government and private interests as a semi-permeable one. It is a one-sided interpretation of the political teaching of classical economics, and in practice represents an unprincipled adaptation to the realities of business lobbying power and the increasing contribution of business funding to political parties. The intellectual rationalisation it uses is a combination of 'rational expectations' and 'public choice' theory, which combine to assert the essential wisdom of firms and the essential folly of government. This argument, which for right-wing theorists is an important motive for bringing private firms into public service, is the following. Competitive success in a perfect market depends in part on having the best possible knowledge, for incorrect knowledge will lead to errors of strategy and eventual bankruptcy. Therefore successful firms can be assumed to have the best possible knowledge, which includes the capacity to anticipate the actions of all other market actors. This is an axiomatic assumption, since it is assumed that in the long run the market ensures the survival of only the fittest – in this case, the firms with the best capacity for acquiring knowledge. No such assumptions can be made about government. It does not exist in a state of perfect competition and therefore has no incentive to act competently. Therefore its knowledge is deeply suspect.

This thesis is used by its more extreme advocates to argue against all government intervention in the economy; if firms in the market necessarily have superior knowledge to government, anything government tries to persuade them to do will be less efficient than what they are doing already. In fact, given their capacity for perfect anticipation, firms will have already worked out what government will be trying to achieve by its intervention and taken evasive action. This perfect knowledge is seen as residing in particular in firms which have achieved successful survival in the financial markets, who deal specifically in economic knowledge, and whose judgement is therefore not open to challenge.

The argument has three practical weaknesses. First, since very many markets are far from perfect, it cannot be assumed that even the most successful firms have honed their knowledge gathering capacities to the highest possible degree. Second, in a rapidly changing world, we cannot ever specify what will actually constitute perfect knowledge after the immediate future; since knowledge acquisition takes time, we cannot assume that any firm has enough knowledge to deal with the longer-term future. During the extended stock-market boom of the 1990s many normally thoughtful people came to believe that somehow the information technology sector had finally solved all such problems. The collapse of that boom during 2000 should serve as a valuable reminder that the knowledge embedded in stock exchanges can be less than perfect.

Both these points suggest that the market does not have automatic superiority over public planning. The third point is stronger: certain forms of knowledge are peculiarly available to centrally located agents (i.e. governments), who are able to acquire knowledge from outside the market process. In other words, while firms may have advantages over governments in some kinds of knowledge acquisition, governments may have the edge in certain other kinds.

Though in practice absurd, this theory has nevertheless exerted a powerful implicit grip over public policy thinking in recent years, to the extent that chronic lack of self-confidence has affected public authorities at all levels. To sustain their self-respect and give themselves any legitimacy at all, they respond by trying to make themselves as much like private firms as possible (e.g. through internal marketisation), by bringing in expertise, consultants and actual service delivery from the private sector, and by privatising to it and generally exposing as much of government (or former government) services as possible to the judgement of the financial markets. Former distinctions between the ethic of public service and that of private profit-making business are necessarily cast aside in such a process. If the wisdom of firms is always superior to that of government, the idea of a proper limit of business influence on government becomes absurd. While these processes were already firmly in place during the Conservative Governments of the 1980s and early 1990s, they have reached a certain climax with New Labour, which, in view of its party's past, feels a particular need to demonstrate its business friendliness. One of the most startling examples of this is the decision to allow individual corporations to place staff members on temporary secondment to ministries. Equally significant is the way in which government has so much lost confidence in its own distinctive contribution that it has allowed even some regulatory activities to be privatised, as we shall see in the following chapter.

This process becomes self-fulfilling. As government contracts out an increasing range of its activities, its employees really do lose competence in the areas being covered by the contractors, areas within which public servants have until now had unrivalled expertise. As they become mere brokers between public principals and private agents, so professional and technical knowledge pass to the latter. Before long it will become an argument in favour of private contractors that only they have the relevant expertise.

In the process of trying to make themselves as similar as possible to private firms, public authorities also have to divest themselves of an intrinsic aspect of their role: the fact that they are authorities, in the sense that they must regulate, and occasionally make decisions which admonish. This loss does not extend to the political centre of national government itself. In fact, far from achieving the disappearance of state power dreamed of by libertarians, the privatising state concentrates power into a tight central nucleus, which deals predominantly with its peer elites in private business. This happens in the following way. Lower and intermediate authorities, in particular local government, have to transform their activities into the purchaser/provider model given by the market. The authority role is therefore sucked out of them. Central government also privatises many of its own functions to consultants and suppliers of various kinds. But there is an irreducible political core which constitutes the elected part of capitalist democracy, which cannot be sold off (though it can be compromised to lobbyists), and which wields the ultimate authority, at least over decisions how and whether to privatise and contract out. This core becomes ever smaller as privatisation progresses, but it cannot be eliminated altogether without a collapse of the concept of both the state and democracy. The more that there is privatisation and a marketisation model for public service delivery, particularly at local level, the more a Jacobin model of centralised democracy and a citizenship without intermediate levels of political action has to be imposed.

The loss of citizenship capacity

There are further, more direct problems for citizens' rights in the models of both privatisation and contracting out. Freedland has drawn attention to the triangular relationship: government, citizen, privatised supplier of services.[6] The citizen has a link, through the electoral and political system, to government (national or local). Government has a link, through the law of contract, with the privatised supplier. But the citizen has no link, neither of market nor of citizenship, to the supplier; as we have noted, service users are not technically customers. And following privatisation they can no longer raise questions of service delivery with government, because it has contracted such delivery away. Henceforth government is responsible only for policy, not for operations.

Freedland wrote before the various railway crises of 2000 and 2001, which demonstrated a further aspect: the sub-contracting chain. Following either privatisation or contracting out, firms further sub-contract elements of their task, and the service moves even further away from citizens' reach. One of the main difficulties in establishing responsibility for railway failure has been the capacity of different sub-contractors in an ever-lengthening chain to lose responsibility in the legal labyrinth of contract terms which links them. A question over service delivery can be untangled only, if at all, in complex litigation.

An important argument in support of contracting out certain elements of health and education provision is that private contractors are already used quite uncontroversially by public service (e.g. government offices buy their stationery in the normal way). This argument becomes particularly strong when linked to contemporary business theory about the value of firms concentrating on their 'core business' and contracting out fringe activities. The general concept of core business is valid and important, and must in fact be used by those who want to insist on the distinctive place of citizenship in the services we are discussing. The citizenship component constitutes the core, and there clearly are 'fringe' components which can be safely hived off without damaging this. The important issue is how the core should be defined. There are two rival approaches: (a) define the core extensively, with a policy priority being to safeguard the needs of public authority and service – which as we have seen includes safeguarding the need for detailed knowledge of the conduct of services by those publicly responsible for them; or (b) maximise privatisation opportunities by defining the core as narrowly as possible. This disregards the needs set out in (a), producing some of the negative results we have been discussing. By committing itself so fully to the attractions of commercialisation, Labour has been effectively adopting option (b).

During the late 1990s and early 2000s many firms decided that their earlier enthusiasm for minimising their definition of the core business, down-sizing and de-layering, had gone too far. They had become dependent on external suppliers who, once they had won a long-term contract, were not always concerned about maximising efficiency. Also, the contracting-out route contradicts another aspect of good business practice: the importance of developing a corporate culture and staff commitment. This is, ironically, particularly important in services rather than manufacturing, there often being little distinction between the personnel and the product in service delivery. Can an organisational ethos be fully maintained if the personnel concerned are the employees of a sub-sub-sub-contractor?

There are therefore major risks in following the contracting out route. Indeed, if we follow the logic of commercialisation to its conclusion, one can envisage the emergence of a quite different idea of politics. By distancing itself from service delivery through lengthy contract chains, government could imitate a discovery of the really smart firms of the 1990s: get rid of the core business itself. Companies found that if all the work of making a product were contracted out, the firm itself could concentrate on the sole task of developing its brand image. The role of the successful firm, liberated from any substantive tasks, became just the development of the brand and its association with fashionable ideas and celebrities – and this, rather than intrinsic product quality, became the key to its sales. This process has been skilfully exposed by Naomi Klein in her book *No Logo*.[7] How much easier would the work of governments be if they needed to cultivate only their brand and image, and were not directly responsible for the actual quality of their policy products!

This leads us in turn to the final answer to the puzzle of what it is that private firms might offer which cannot be provided from within the public service itself: presentation. Public service professionals tend to neglect presentation to a fault; their distinctive ethic tells them to concentrate on the quality of the service itself. Politicians themselves, although they are part of the public sector, inhabit a world far closer to that of the private sector, as they are constantly having to sell themselves and increasingly do so through packaging and media 'spin' rather than by ensuring substantive quality. It is a small step to the realisation that the growth of the presentation approach within these services could remove the public gaze from their actual quality and focus it on the advertising schemes that private firms bring with them.

The logical conclusion to this process would then be a 'fully spun' political world where health, education and other services would continue to be central to political debate, but where that debate took the form of rival efforts at branding, just as most television advertisements refer somewhere to a product but are primarily concerned with associating that product with certain images that have nothing to do with its intrinsic qualities. Electoral competition in such a context would no doubt continue to be intense and creative, as rival parties sought to associate themselves with winning imagery – but it would be a competition detached from the awkward facts of real life.

I am not suggesting that such a world is the aim of today's politicians, but it can be seen as the ultimate destination towards which the processes of commercialisation are leading. Once governments have sub-contracted their services to elongated supply chains of private firms, they will no more be responsible for their production than Nike is for making the shoes it brands. If one runs this scenario through the Freedland triangle, one sees that citizens would lose virtually all capacity to translate their concerns into political action. Elections would then become games around brands, rather than opportunities for citizens to talk back to politicians about the quality of services. Extreme though this might seem, it is only an extension of a process with which we have become so familiar that we no longer even notice it: the approximation of the democratic electoral process, the highest expression of citizenship rights, to a marketing campaign based quite openly on the manipulative techniques used to sell products.

In fact the alarm bells should be ringing well before that final stage is reached. For once public services are treated in most respects as commodities just like any other, how much longer will it be possible to defend their being subsidised and not bought and sold in the market like other commodities too? How long will the current taboo on full privatisation then last? The Prime Minister has recently suggested that the next stage of reform is 'co-payment' for public services – that is, private consumer fees.[8] It seems that we may already be on that path.

2 | The case of education

School-level education has been a policy field where the contradictions between citizenship and commercialisation approaches have been particularly clear in government policy. The concept of citizenship entitlement is highly developed in education. Partly because so much of its provision is compulsory, partly because in a democracy all political parties are required to advocate opportunities for social mobility, there is an almost universal expectation that education should be available as a right, not needing to be purchased in the market – though in practice in the UK and some other countries this ideal has always been heavily compromised by the existence of fee-paying schools to which many wealthy people send their children.

The strong element of compulsion exists because, if having their children educated was voluntary, many parents would fail to do so. This would create problems of social order and might weaken the eventual economic capacity of these children. It is therefore difficult to apply one fundamental attribute of the market, freedom of consumer choice. It would be even more difficult to apply the other fundamental attribute: the payment of prices which reflect the production costs of the good or service offered. If this were applied, even fewer parents would have their children educated, or they would buy very cheap and inadequate schooling. In principle compulsory consumption could be combined with all other attributes of the market: parents could be left free to choose from a range of private school suppliers, and to pay fees. There would however be severe political objections to enforced payment of private consumption. Education presents particularly difficult problems for a full application of market logic – which would mean treating it like any other good, offered for sale according to supply and demand – without distorting and degrading the service provided.

Markets and private firms therefore hover on the margins of the compulsory education system, in two main forms: the introduction of market analogues without privatisation into the school admissions system; and the contracting out of educational services, including increasingly the teaching of subjects in schools, to firms. Both will be explored below.

Making markets in education

For parents and their children, the choice of school which a child will attend is the most market-like aspect of the education system. Governments eager to introduce elements of the market have therefore concentrated attention on extending parents' freedom of choice in this field. However, for the reasons outlined above, they have had to do this without use of the price mechanism. This limits heavily the degree of marketisation that can be introduced, as it eliminates two fundamental roles of price within a true market: as a unitary indicator which is considered to summarise all relevant qualities of an item of the good in question, enabling it to be compared with rivals and facilitating choice; and as a rationing device for distribution. Governments have found solutions to these deficiencies. However, the result has been, not a happy compromise creating something new between citizenship and markets, but a dysfunctional stalemate.

The problem of the absence of price as a quality indicator can in principle be tackled by constructing analogues to guide customers, and doing this has been a major element of policy. The main solution found by the Conservative Government and continued by Labour has been the introduction of official tests of pupils' performance, administered at ages seven, eleven, fourteen and sixteen. The results of these are published and used to rank and compare schools. Parents are encouraged to use them as indicators of quality when choosing schools for their children. At the same time, schools' performances in the annual GCSE and A Level GCE examinations are calculated, ranked and widely published in the press. All this facilitates a market-like process, but it has two principal defects which may distort educational provision.

First, partial indicators encourage schools to maximise performance on those items reflected in the indicators alone. If success in certain examinations is measured and published, the rational school will concentrate on those at the expense of other activities. There have been many examples of this, leading to demands that government adjust the indicators used so that they cover all relevant areas, and government has been responsive to these pleas. But there are two limitations to this strategy. First, if indicators multiply, they become too complex, and people find them difficult to appraise. As Onora O'Neill observed in the third of her 2002 BBC Reith Lectures, as targets become more and more technical and complex, and are changed with increasing frequency, the 'public' ceases to be able to understand them at all.[9] The new accountability is not to the public at all, but just to the political centre. Second, as she also observed, the vast volume of work involved in record keeping and target-making means that the attention of professionals is increasingly focussed on these, giving them less time for genuine engagement with the real public, their clients.

A second and highly contentious issue has been the use of pupils' performance as a judgement on school quality, when it is well known that children's academic achievements depend heavily on their social background. The Labour Government initiated a system of baseline testing to reflect this: children are tested on entry to a school; subsequent test performances can then be compared with their initial achievements to assess the value added by the school. The White Paper that eventually became the Education Act 2002 announced that indicators based on these baseline results will eventually be published alongside – but not instead of – the raw data. But many parents may be more interested in the raw data. They want to know both what the school achieves and the quality of its raw material, for in this way they can select schools with suitable fellow pupils for their children. The indicator system sends signals which can be used to reinforce social segregation. In any case, as Brighouse has pointed out, general school measures tell parents very little about the particular balance of characteristics that they seek for their child.[10]

Test scores have not been the only forms of quality signal developed by governments to make markets for school choice. Further indicators are provided by the reports of Ofsted, the Office for Standards in Education, introduced by the Conservatives to give more impetus to change and higher public prominence to school inspection than the school visits of HM Inspectorate of Schools. Ofsted grades schools into various categories, including the highly negative ones of 'having serious weaknesses', or 'requiring special measures' to improve them.

A further technique has been the development of different types of school. In some parts of the country the old 1944 system of a distinction between grammar schools and residual schools was never abolished, and New Labour has no objection to this situation continuing. The Conservative Education Reform Act

1988 had provided for the establishment of Grant Maintained Schools (GMS). To encourage schools to become GMSs the Government introduced certain inducements, such as generous capital and other grants which were not available to LEA schools. GMSs were permitted to select up to 15 per cent of their pupils from outside their catchment areas, using whatever criteria they liked. GMS status therefore served as a signal to parents that this was a school in favoured financial circumstances and to some extent able to recruit pupils of its choice – a strong market signal.

In practice the implications of this policy were limited: not many GMSs were introduced; their distribution through the country was very uneven. Their contribution to increased choice and to a market in schools was therefore small, arbitrary and sometimes negative. Further extensions of this experiment were stopped by the Labour Government of 1997, which also changed the status of existing GMSs to that of foundation schools; for many purposes, including the crucial question of admissions, they were brought back under LEA responsibility.

However, at secondary level Labour also embarked on an alternative policy of its own for inserting new forms of school within the state system but possessing attractive qualities which would mark them out from ordinary schools. The 2001 White Paper proposed a major expansion of the existing experimental policy of 'specialist schools'. These seek to develop expertise in certain particular kinds of education – such as technology, arts, sports, business studies. To help them fulfil their particular mission, they will be able to select up to 10 per cent of their pupils based on ability within their chosen specialisms. The Government intends that 40 per cent of all secondary schools in England should be 'specialist' by 2005, with a further group in the category of 'working towards' specialist status. (The Government has now said that ultimately it wants all schools to have some kind of specialism.) In addition to LEAs, voluntary bodies, religious organisations and private firms can apply for the right to establish them. In addition to their limited selection right, specialist schools will have the right to pay teachers more than other schools. Schools which have been successful specialist schools for five years will have the chance to become advanced specialist schools, receiving more funding than those around them but also having some responsibilities to develop materials and training and provide services for these others.

The Government argues that specialist schools do not mark a return to selection, because a diversity of specialisms will be recognised, not just general academic ability, and no school is prohibited from working towards specialist status. It is in fact more concerned to make markets than intensify selection, the emphasis of the arguments of the White Paper being on expanding diversity in order to increase choice. However, since superior funding and privileges are to be a mark of specialist schools, it is clear that they are being marked out as more desirable, and not just diverse.

The White Paper introduced a further distinction among schools in its concept of the 'successful' school, formal criteria for defining which will be devised. Under certain conditions 'successful' schools might be permitted: to pay higher salaries to their teachers; to be exempted for teaching parts of the National Curriculum; and to expand their size irrespective of local admissions and school size policies.

The Conservative Education Reform Act 1988, which introduced the tests and the Ofsted model, concomitantly gave parents increased rights to choose individual schools within their local authority, rather than being allocated to their neighbouring school. Schools were then given incentives to attract parents, as they were rewarded financially if they could compete successfully with their neighbours in recruiting pupils. Labour retained all these policies and, as we have seen above, is strengthening some of the mechanisms which divert pupils numbers and resources to certain schools.

Together all these policies over the 1988 to 2001 period have put in place a powerful market analogue whereby customers (parents) are equipped with information to find the most successful schools, and providers (schools) have strong incentives to attract customers. This might seem to be a highly desirable situation, but it has a number of negative consequences. If, as the 2001 White Paper implies, all that is happening is that diversity is being expanded so that customers with different tastes can find providers to match, there would be little to worry about, apart from a large number of minor frictions when supply and demand for particular school characteristics did not match in certain areas. In reality however it is not a question of a wide diversity, but a ranking of 'good' and 'bad' schools. Test and examination results, Ofsted reports, the eventual designations of 'successful' schools all point in the same direction. In theory specialist schools will cover a wider range of attributes, but many of them will be 'specialising' in those areas of the curriculum which deliver the high test scores. Clearly, demand for these will exceed supply. In a true market the price of 'good' schools would rise to bring demand and supply into equilibrium. But this second, controversial role of price as a means of rationing is ruled out by the citizenship principles of the national education system.

The market approach therefore has to operate without substantive prices. In doing this however it does not produce a compromise, but continues to violate citizenship principles. As 'good' or popular schools use their additional resources to expand, 'poor' schools, starved of both pupils and resources, will necessarily decline, and will either eventually close or be left with a residuum of children whose parents do not care. Alternatively, poor schools, shaken out of their complacency as the spiral of decline envelops them, will make determined attempts to improve. In doing this they have an uphill task, as resources and pupils continue to haemorrhage from them.

If nearly all pupils end up in the successful schools while the poor schools decline, there are further negative components. It is a long, slow process. Schools cannot expand quickly, and during that period whole cohorts of children will pass through helplessly declining schools. It is also possible for schools to grow too big to continue with their current regimes; a successful school might be undermined by its very expansion. Further, in many parts of the country the closure of some schools and the removal of pupils to a different one imposes high transport costs on children, which government is already reluctant to meet.

But more insidious than these problems is a perverse analogue of a school fee which emerges when elements of the market are introduced into a theoretically non-selective system. If the supply of places in 'good' schools cannot rise to meet demand, there is competition among parents. This competition is resolved in ways which cannot be reconciled with the citizenship model. Schools' achievements are determined by two factors: the initial cultural capital that pupils bring with them (the quality of the raw materials) and the quality of the education which the school provides (the school's added value). While parents are 'customers', their children are the raw materials which are fashioned by the school to produce the end product. The customers thus make their own contribution to their children's schools' performance, and hence to the schools' ability to acquire resources. Schools therefore have an incentive to admit children from parents likely to contribute strong social capital and to reject those who lack cultural capital. Children's educational potential therefore serves as a curious analogue of a school fee within the new price analogue system; the higher the ability of a child, the better chances its parents have of acquiring the school

33

place they wanted; and the higher the subsequent 'profits' of the school. If this process proceeds unchecked, inequalities of achievement between schools which attract the 'best' pupils because of their own past record, and those which are unable to do so, will spiral. The quality of education of those in unfavoured schools will deteriorate. Any role which schools might play as channels of social mobility will be completely undermined.

The citizenship approach to these problems first limits schools' ability to choose their pupils in order to reduce the onset of the spiral of inequality; and second and more important takes direct action of various kinds to improve education quality in poor schools. The market and citizenship approaches are here mutually incompatible. The former works by using parental choice to encourage inequalities between schools to accumulate, and then redistributes resources from poor to successful schools. The citizenship approach tries to limit the destabilising effects on schools of parental choice, redistributes resources to poor schools, and takes many direct action measures to improve their performance.

Contradictory though they are, the Labour Government seeks to honour simultaneously the citizenship model and the new marketisation strategy. Since 1997 it has undertaken many measures for directly improving poor schools, and *Schools – Achieving Success* set out further strong and imaginative new policies for doing the same. The 2002 Green Paper proposed a number of measures for recognising vocational forms of education alongside academic ones – though in doing so it threatened even more complex indicators and measures of performance. But the 2001 White Paper had sustained and even reinforced all elements of the market analogue approach which constantly undermine the efforts of these schools to improve by encouraging parents with strong cultural capital to avoid them. Additional resources will be steered towards both successful schools and those experiencing particular difficulties; both specialist schools and those in areas of deprivation will be able to offer higher pay to help them recruit the best teachers. Every help offered to schools with problems is counteracted by an equivalent help offered to the privileged. There is little to prevent many of the former becoming residual schools for children unable to find a place in either a specialist school of some kind or a residentially favoured comprehensive; and somewhere in the middle there will be schools excluded from both contradictory redistributive flows. The solution held out by the White Paper for resolving these dilemmas was to increase the number of specialist schools and aspirants to that status, in order to ensure that they are not just a small elite. But the more that this is done, the more extreme is the ghetto to which the residual schools are consigned.

In many policy areas, in particular those concerned with the distribution of income, it has been made clear that New Labour's concept of egalitarianism means trying to move the lowest percentiles of the population closer to the median, while remaining unconcerned that the distance between the median and the top percentiles is increasing. The schools policy of the 2001 White Paper is a perfect example of this philosophy: it is concerned to ensure that the lowest percentiles achieve higher standards than they do at present, while creating mechanisms for ensuring that the upper percentiles move even further ahead. As a policy for increasing the all-round educational performance of the national workforce, this is entirely coherent. However, as a policy for securing equality of opportunity it cannot escape its internal contradictions. To the extent that competition for good jobs is a zero-sum game, the mechanisms of parental and school choice analysed above ensure that improving further the quality of schools available to those with most cultural capital wipes out any compensatory measures taken to help poor schools.

The distortion and residualisation of LEAs

The market analogue model and the prominence of league tables gives even schools which do not have official selection possibilities strong incentives to try to get the 'best' children, and equally to avoid the 'worst'. There are numerous ways in which they can do this, such as trying to dissuade parents of poorly performing children from choosing them, or by excluding children with behaviour problems and passing them on to neighbouring schools. Schools' admissions and catchment area practices have to be strongly policed if this kind of 'black market' in school places is to be avoided, a policing which becomes more necessary as marketisation grows. However, Conservative and Labour Governments have instead weakened the available policing mechanisms, mainly through the weakening of local education authorities which has itself been a major aspect of the marketisation strategy. Indeed, in 2001 a consultation document issued alongside *Schools – Achieving Success*, acknowledged explicitly that a free market in admissions was simply not working, and that LEAs would in future play a stronger co-ordinating role. Once again the Government's citizenship agenda had clashed with its marketisation one. There was not however a clear change back to the former; again the Government is simultaneously pursuing contradictory approaches. Stressing the co-ordinating role of LEAs runs alongside, but does not replace, the recent history of their general disempowerment.

First, both Conservative and Labour Governments have marketised LEAs' relationship to schools, changing it from one of a monitoring authority to that of a supplier of commercial services. Second, and consequent on this, Labour has sought to replace them at as many points as possible by private firms. These policies in themselves threaten major distortions and an eventual residualisation of LEAs.

An initial major requirement for transforming relations

between schools and LEAs into market analogues was a distortion of the organisational character of schools themselves. Producers in markets are firms, who have to buy the labour and raw materials they use to make their products. To fit this, schools have had to be changed from their historical model as organisations sui generis, to increasingly resemble small firms.

First, the Education Act 1986 (No 2) introduced the local management of schools (LMS) system, which granted increased decision-making powers to schools. Then the Education Reform Act 1988 removed schools' earlier autonomy over the curriculum through the introduction of a National Curriculum, replacing this with new autonomy in finance and management. Schools, and especially their heads, lost professional autonomy but acquired financial autonomy, encouraging them to see this business-type, non-educational role as their primary self-definition. Head teachers were further encouraged to see themselves as managers, distinct from the teachers who work for them rather than primi inter pares within a teaching profession, by the introduction of performance-related pay for classroom teachers by the Labour Government in 2000. Heads have the job, with external commercial assessors, of deciding on the allocation of performance increments to their staff. They have also been forced to become managers and bureaucrats instead of education professionals by the extraordinary number of short-term, soft-money opportunities which government offers schools as it attempts to sustain a high public profile with more and more initiatives.[11]

In 2001 the Government initiated a policy of encouraging takeovers of unpopular schools by a more popular neighbour as an approach to the problem of inequalities between schools. Significantly it did not use normal professional or local government mechanisms for this – such as the administrative amalgamations already in place and often used by LEAs needing to reduce the number of schools in an area – but the model of the corporate takeover: the acquiring school acts through a commercial acquisition of assets.

While schools have in these ways been persuaded to conceive of themselves as firms, the relationship between them and LEAs has become one of purchasers and providers of educational support services, with LEAs gradually becoming just one among a number of potential providers. This policy was initiated by the Conservatives, but in general during that period LEAs were successful in retaining their role. The main difficulties they faced were that if a school chose to become a GMS, it moved completely outside the LEA's sphere, and funds notionally allocated to the LEA for its administrative support were transferred to the school. Head teachers were therefore able to use the threat of encouraging their governors to consider 'going GMS' as a deterrent to any attempts by an authority to express disagreement with whatever heads were doing.

While the Labour Government had abolished the GMS possibility, it never acknowledged how the existence of GMSs had destroyed LEAs' authority, but took advantage of that weakness to accuse them of not having asserted authority, and used that to justify undermining it even further. During the first two years after 1997 the Government seemed to contemplate abolishing LEAs. This in itself encouraged some head teachers to regard them as of no consequence. But more important have been the Government's substantive policies for further weakening LEAs' authority.

These have been motivated by the exceptional priority that it has placed on moving private sector suppliers into public services. At first, Labour's dominant rhetoric was solely that of LEA failure; it was taken as axiomatic that, while public organisations were likely to fail, private firms delivered consistent success. Certain authorities were deemed to have failed, and private firms given the contract to do their job. This happened to Hackney,

Islington, Liverpool, Sheffield, Leeds, Rotherham, Waltham Forest and Bradford. In all but one case, private firms (rather than action within the public sector) were the solution sought, though in one of these the private intervention itself later failed and was replaced by renewed public involvement. In November 1999 the then schools minister, Estelle Morris, predicted that a further fifteen LEAs would be found to have failed, leading to suspicions that the Government had a privatisation target.[12] In the event the longer list never materialised.

The failure model was also applied to individual schools. The Conservative-controlled Surrey County Council began this in 1998, when it offered the contract to manage a failing school to a private firm. Contrary to widespread expectations that the Government would oppose such a policy, it applauded it. The Education Act 2002 extended the Surrey model by giving the Secretary of State the right to require a local authority to offer a failing school to a private company.

However, private education firms were not interested in being confined to a role of rescuing 'failures', which can be a difficult task, but wanted chances to run profitable services. The ability to 'cherry-pick', to spot where the profitable options are, is fundamental to the entrepreneurial skill of firms who bid for government contracts.

Government responded to the lobbying, but this required a change of policy towards LEAs and a different rhetoric from that of privatisation in the case of their failure. A kind of halfway house had been the policy of Education Action Zones (EAZs), which retained the idea of private firms helping with areas of social difficulty, but in co-operation with LEAs. Government was willing to invest additional resources in areas with specified social problems, provided LEAs found partners from private business to join them, who would be willing to provide 25 per cent of total funding and contribute some form of expertise. The management of schools within an EAZ ceases to be accountable to the LEA, and the business partners are able to influence the curriculum. A similar policy has been the 'city academies' whereby private sponsors can establish schools with innovative curricula freed from some of the constraints of the national curriculum. This might or might not be done in conjunction with the LEA. These experiments have been less confrontational towards LEAs, but maintained the ideology that the private sector held the answer to poor educational performance.

By 2000 Labour was developing from this a completely new, positive strategy of using LEAs themselves as active participants in the search for opportunities for commercialisation. Authorities which co-operated in this were held up for praise; additional finance was made available if they would participate in experiments that might lead to hiving off some of their services. The criteria applied by Ofsted in its inspections of LEAs rewarded those which had structured themselves in a way amenable to piecemeal commercialisation. (Ofsted inspectors often work for firms who will be seeking privatisation contracts.) Then, during the 2001 general election campaign the Prime Minister turned the rhetoric up a further notch: bringing private contractors into the public education and health services became an indicator – indeed, the indicator – of commitment to modernisation. In his subsequent statements on public service reform, 'modernisation' has become a virtual synonym for bringing in the private sector.

LEAs were now in a full Catch-22; failure to succeed made them vulnerable to privatisation; they could demonstrate their commitment to success by being willing to privatise. The Education department invented a new term to describe the new process. LEAs were to be the 'brokers' of services to schools, with the responsibility of creating open markets for these services.[13]

The Conservatives had initiated a policy of compulsory competitive tendering, whereby many services provided directly by local government, such as street cleaning and refuse collection, had to be offered to private contractors, and could be retained by the public service only if it succeeded in under-bidding the competition – usually by worsening the terms of employment of employees. None of this concerned LEAs' core business. This was finally hit through Labour's policy of 'Best Value' reviews. Council departments are required to compare their own structure of service provision throughout the range of activities with those of other authorities, with an emphasis on seeking opportunities for bringing in commercial suppliers. A further instrument has been the New Models project under which government established eleven partnerships between LEAs and a small number of private firms. Some projects comprised consortia of a number of LEAs and a firm, others matched individual LEAs and firms. One, which involved a partnership between an LEA and a book shop chain, giving the latter privileged rights to disseminate schools information in the area, collapsed early. In the other experiments, in principle the authorities and the private firm discuss how the LEAs' services are organised and carried out. This might facilitate subsequent bids by the firm to take over certain services; it certainly puts it in a very privileged place with important inside knowledge.

Converting the services which LEAs provide to schools into commercial ones does not necessarily distort them; there is no reason to regard the cutting of grass in school playing fields or the purchase of exercise books as any different from equivalent transactions by any other organisation. Distortions appear if the character of the service offered is adversely changed by being forced into a commercial mould. This does happen where the distinctive position of LEAs' work as the exercise of public authority and professional judgement is concerned, and yet this kind of work has in no way been excluded from the government's privatisation attempts. The Best Value reviews and New

41

Models experiments provide strong examples of this. These operate by redefining the LEA activities concerned as though they were indistinguishable from any kind of service provided for customers by a firm. This is necessary, because if LEA functions are viewed in their actually existing form as the exercise of professional monitoring authority on behalf of a public interest, it would be LEAs who would appear as having the superior experience and capacity.

Some of the resulting distortions are merely silly – as when targets for 'customer satisfaction' are sought in the number of parental preferences in school choice met, or in reductions in the number of appeals made over school admissions decisions. These outcomes depend heavily on the behaviour of individual schools and, in many cases, the character of the areas in which schools are located, rather than in any deliberate actions by LEA staff. More important is the way in which treating admissions services as a marketable customer service ignores the issues discussed above: conflict between schools, their desire to improve their pupil base, to try exclude children from 'difficult' estates, and to pass disruptive pupils on to rivals through exclusions. Dealing with these and similar issues requires a policing rather than a service-supplier role.

Initially the positive arguments for contracting out had used the 'core business' argument, but this changed. For some years the Government had acknowledged the non-commercialisable character of many 'core' decisions made by LEA staff, and therefore limited hiving off to routine tasks only; but this changed as its determination to maximise privatisation intensified. In spring 2001 a simple Order of the then Department for Education and Skills extended the range of services which LEAs ought to consider privatising to include those affecting authorities' exercise of 'discretion'. This mainly concerns judgements in individual children's cases. A small list of LEA functions remains still excluded from contracting out, but these are largely restricted to formal, budget-setting tasks, not educational ones. By the time of *Schools – Achieving Success*, Government saw no reason why schools should not contract out various lessons or subjects to private companies, or LEAs their school improvement work. The public education service now no longer has a core business, which means that none of its activities are considered unsuitable for commercialisation.

The likely outcome of this process will be not just the distortions of LEAs' role discussed so far, but their residualisation. Firms are explicitly mentioned as eligible to seek to establish specialist schools. Given that many LEAs are likely to have severe reservations about the highly controversial specialist school concept, that it is the Government who will decide on the establishment of such schools, and that Government is eagerly seeking ways of increasing private sector involvement in school provision, it is probable that a high proportion of specialist schools will be run by firms. Some advanced specialist schools will also be privately run, receiving additional government subsidy and a favoured chance of selling services to other schools in their area. The 2001 White Paper envisaged ensuring a major role for private firms in the establishment of new schools everywhere. Henceforth, when an LEA identifies the need for a new school, it must do all the preparatory work, including finding a site. At that point however it must invite bids to build and run the school from voluntary and religious groups and commercial firms. The Secretary of State will have the sole right to select the successful bidder. Again, given the Government's preferences, it is likely to grant a high number of these to the commercial sector.

In time private firms will come to own a large share of the privileged specialist schools, and in general the newest and best equipped schools, leaving the public sector to make good the obligation of universal provision by filling the gaps rejected as unprofitable. There are signs that the Government is consciously preparing such an outcome. It has been encouraging a model whereby local authority education departments are amalgamated with social services departments. The latter are mainly concerned with services of social repair and casualties – especially in the case of children's services, the only part of social services work that touches the same client group as education. Education departments can only be sensibly merged with social services departments if the former have also become primarily services for social casualties. Virtually the only role in the direct provision of education reserved to LEAs by the 2002 Education Act is that of running full-time, out-of-school pupil referral units in which an attempt must be made to educate pupils excluded from all the schools of their area because of their behaviour. The numbers of such pupils must be expected to rise, as the Act will also make it easier for head teachers permanently to exclude children; and private firms can be expected to want to exclude such pupils from the schools under their control.

It is a well established finding of occupational sociology that there is high morale among staff involved in experiment and innovation, while that of those who know that they are engaged in an activity which is being run down declines. Private firms taking over the running of schools in the USA have often been able to show results superior to the existing public sector. The staff involved in these novelties are likely to feel a boost to their morale in comparison with colleagues labouring away in an increasingly residual public service. In addition, the firm itself devotes high-quality senior staff and close attention to these experimental cases; they are 'loss leaders', being abnormally highly funded in order to win new contracts. The only fair comparison with an experimental, heavily resourced private experiment would be with a similar experiment taking place wholly within the public system, not with the routine mass.

The Government has also been trying to restrict the role of LEAs' advisory services, which advise schools on best practice, identify weaknesses, and assist schools with difficulties in meeting their teaching objectives. They have been told to restrict their activities to cases where schools are clearly in difficulties, and not to spend time with schools that are functioning well.[14] A private market is developing whereby firms of consultants give such advice, and they prefer to work with successful schools, which are in any case more likely to have resources to spend on their services. By being restricted to contacts with problem schools LEA advisors will not only lose their chance to act pro-actively and identify early weaknesses appearing in currently successful ones, but they will lose contact with best practice developing in the best schools. This latter will become a monopoly preserve of the private firms, and LEA staff will again be suitable only for dealing with casualties.

A very important theme of central government criticism of local government during Labour's first few years of office was the neglect of 'joined up government' – the need for particular departments and units to integrate their work with others. Considerable use was also made of the virtues of the 'one-stop shop' – such as the ability of parents or schools to get most of the information they needed from an LEA from a single known source. These desiderata become increasingly difficult to achieve if various parts of an LEA's services have been commercialised, and if former colleagues now have to relate to each other across a barrier erected by the terms of a purchaser/provider service contract. It is also difficult to secure services from a provider which have not been anticipated in advance in the terms of a contract. Contract terms necessarily trump any need to respond to newly emerging needs or to innovate in tackling problems. Performing the professional task is displaced and the substantive goals of the education service are distorted.

More generally, the more services that an LEA contracts out, the more its staff lose detailed, day-to-day knowledge about its schools. Information that previously passed between colleagues within the same organisation again has to cross the purchaser/provider boundary. Some information will become the private property of the firm, and LEA staff may have to pay to have access to it. This imposes rigidities, as it is difficult to predict all future information needs at the time a contract is being drawn up. Since so much of the knowledge needed for the day-to-day running of a system is informal, even tacit, it can in no way be defined in a contract and purchased.

The exclusion of LEAs from future-oriented roles goes further. In 2001 the Government established a Learning and Skills Council (LSC), to have responsibility for all sixteen-nineteen year old, adult and community education. Its members are appointed by central government, and it will itself appoint the members of its 47 local councils; there will be no guaranteed LEA representation, though the LSC and its local bodies will have a duty to consult them.[15] All education institutions providing for these levels, including school sixth forms, will henceforth receive their funds from the LSC and not from LEAs, though the latter's staff will still have to do the clerical work involved in the transactions. This begins a process of removing LEAs from involvement with sixth-form education, a crucial part of the school system. In 2002 the process was taken even further, when the Government announced that the role of (and funding by) the LSC could move down to age fourteen.

LEAs are today expected to retain a small and continuously declining proportion of their funding for their own services, distributing the rest to schools. Meanwhile, in addition to their continuing duties, they have to use these funds to respond to increasing demands from government to work on special projects, much of it related to privatisation. The sums left to them for their own pro-active activities are becoming tiny – which makes it easier to stigmatise them as not being at the cutting edge. Almost the only chances they have of acquiring resources for innovation are to bid for participation in government special projects, which almost always require working with a private partner. This not only strengthens a stereotype of LEAs innovating only when associated with such partners; it also forces even authorities which are hostile to such relationships to undertake them, giving an impression of active support.

In all these developments we see the contradiction between the market and citizenship. Marketisation involves contracting out to private firms those things which they consider that they can make profitable. This 'cherry-picking' is an essential attribute of the successful government contractor – and it takes us to the heart of the main reason why the private sector often seems more efficient than the public. But the citizenship ideal requires education to be a universal service, which means that someone has to do the unprofitable work. Under a marketisation model this is the task of the residual public service. But residual provision is a betrayal of universal citizenship.

Privatisation before marketisation

The use of market analogues in school admissions and the commercialisation of LEA services and school management are separate policies, but they relate to each other at two points. First, as we have seen, the more that LEAs are commercialised - either by full privatisation or by themselves acting according to commercial criteria – the less they are able to play the authority role in relation to schools which the latter's marketisation requires if abuses are to be checked. Second, while 'cherry-picking' is central to market behaviour, elements of the way in which it is being conducted raise doubts about whether the current policy represents a true move to markets. We are here contending with distortions, not caused by the market, but of the market itself.

The conversion of a citizenship service into a commercial one alongside surviving citizenship assumptions requires such an extensive upheaval in its character that not only the service itself, but the markets which develop, themselves become distorted. They have to be politically fixed, and in the process some of the positive qualities associated with markets are lost. These distortions began under the Conservatives, but either because they lost office when the process was still in early stages of development, or because they believed that entrepreneurs would simply appear if space was created for them, they did not make much progress in shaping markets and directly encouraging entrepreneurs into the education arena. This task has therefore fallen primarily to Labour.

A major advantage of market provision proposed by its advocates is that the market is anonymous and not vulnerable to political manipulation. However, the difficulty of constructing markets in the education sector means that government becomes involved in an intensive lobbying process with a small number of key players. Since this has been happening during a period when central government's relations with local government have been cooling, a small number of firms have enjoyed a far closer political relationship to ministers than have local authorities, despite the party and civil service links apparently connecting different levels of government. Central government has consistently maintained a distance from LEAs, and is residualising their role in schools, as we have seen.

Not surprisingly, therefore, the various initiatives discussed above have presented firms with very attractive terms. For example, when they or others run city academies, they must pay 20 per cent of capital costs, but ownership of the land and buildings is transferred to them from local government without charge. When, in July 2001, a semi-private City Technology College in Nottingham was enabled to acquire the lease of a neighbouring, under-subscribed comprehensive, additional government funding was released to improve the school, which would not have been available had the school stayed in local authority hands. Design of the Payment By Results (PBR) system for teachers was contracted in 1999 for £3 million, without competitive tendering, to a firm, Hay McBer, while a second firm, Cambridge Education Associates, was given the £100 million five-year contract for running the system.[16] (The firm employs more than 3,000 assessors to check head teachers' assessments of their staff.)[17] LEAs were not even consulted about operation of the PBR scheme.

There have also been instances of permitting firms to brand educational activities in schools. The Learning and and Skills Development Agency has funded a GNVQ pack devoted to the study of one firm – Legoland.[18] Materials advertising Legoland are included in the packs. Less dramatically, it is already virtually routine for individual IT firms to be granted monopoly contracts, heavily subsidised by public funds, to provide information technology services to schools and other public organisations; the receiving organisation is then completely dependent on that firm's practices (and prices) as it introduces product modifications which may make the initial installation redundant.

In the USA and Canada it is already commonplace for schools to base their teaching programmes around the image and products of an individual corporation. In exchange for sponsorship, firms can acquire monopoly rights over access to children in their schools, or can impose wearing of clothes bearing their logos as a form of school uniform, or even require that children watch advertisements on their school computer screens for a certain period of time each day. Would central government now raise any objections to the expansion of such practices in the UK? Does it have any concept of either the appropriate limits of the reach of commercialisation, or of the dangers of granting individual firms monopoly privileges, which conflict with the idea of the free market?

Contract-winning as the new core education business

Non-market approaches to private sector involvement are very dominant in the new policies for commercialisation of citizenship services. Because the Government is not sure how to commercialise these areas, it wants information from insiders. Because it is desperate to maximise this new role of the private sector, it wants to make its offers to private firms as attractive as possible. It is therefore eagerly vulnerable to intensive lobbying by firms who see major opportunities of soft profits.

The Labour Government itself has sometimes been tough with contractors, for example imposing penalty clauses in contracts if they fail to deliver improved standards in schools which they take over. It could perhaps give greater guidance to local government staff on how to drive hard bargains in contract negotiations with private sector firms. To date all responsibility for educating LEAs in private-public partnerships seems to have been delegated to the firms themselves, who are unlikely to include this among their lessons.

The overall approach is courting the worst of two worlds, with both marketisation and citizenship losing out, not this time because of a clash between them, but because both clash with the practice of insider lobbying and preferred bidders. This approach runs all the risks of service deterioration of commercialisation discussed above, without the advantages – keen pricing, genuine choice for ultimate consumers – which the true market can often bring. It carries all the disadvantages of state involvement in commercial transactions – the formation of privileged circles of suppliers – without the restraining hand of the public service ethos which has been discarded in favour of a commercial one. Although the whole exercise is being carried out using the rhetoric of free-market economics, in reality it returns us to the world of relations between government and monopoly-holding 'court favourites' against which Adam Smith and others developed their initial formulations of that economics.

Government contracts within the commercialising welfare state are very attractive. As we have already noted, they are necessarily long-term – as much as 25 to 30 years in the case of buildings, such as schools. It would in fact be very difficult for, say, an LEA to contract out management of its school admissions services to a different firm every year or two, as the learning curves involved in getting to know the district and its schools would impose considerable inefficiencies. This process makes it very difficult to deal with dissatisfaction with the quality of a service being offered. Also, during a seven-year period a contractor can expect to develop very close relations with personnel in the contracting authority, making it a highly privileged insider when the contract eventually comes up for renewal.

Furthermore, in its eagerness to commercialise, the government has heavily subsidised most of these developments. For example, government invested £1.8 million in the New Models projects, most of which money went to private firms, though most of the work for the experiments was carried out by LEAs. The information flow within the projects is entirely unidirectional. The firm learns everything it wants about how the LEAs work and about their finances; they are told nothing equivalent about the firm operates. It is then in a good position to bid to take over selected parts of the LEAs' work. The firms are in effect being subsidised in their attempts to secure profit-making contracts.

The character of the firms which have entered the new market is instructive. A number have emerged specifically around it. Their founders have usually been former teachers or LEA staff who saw the chances of higher incomes by going private at a time when the Government has been cutting expenditure on administration within public service, but subsidising higher spending on it if the same services are provided privately. These firms draw almost entirely on existing LEA staff for the personnel with which they will replace such staff if they win a contract.

Other participants in the market are firms which have lengthy histories in other economic sectors, and which have developed education service branches in response to government encouragement: for example, Arthur Andersen and PriceWaterhouseCoopers, both accountancy and management consultancy specialists; Group 4, security services and private prisons specialists; W.S. Atkins, an earlier spin-off of commercialised local government building and other services. Serco, experienced in missile warning systems, private prisons and young offenders' institutions, acquired QAA, a school inspection firm, in late 2000. Amey Roadstone, primarily a highways construction corporation, has linked up with Nord-Anglia, a specialist education firm.[19] These companies all have prior widespread experience of and success in how to win government contracts of various kinds. They have highly developed lobbying resources in Whitehall and Westminster and extensive contacts within government. It is these attributes which have given them their past success in winning government contracts, and which have encouraged them to enter the new sector of commercialised public education services, the substantive business of which is quite new to them. This is arguably the only added value which they bring to the education system. It is the value of the Whitehall insider, a value which is relevant to the delivery of education only because Government has decided to contract out; it is therefore not a quality which constitutes a reason for contracting-out in the first place or which delivers anything to the ultimate consumer of the services.

The risks inherent in this system of privileged contract insiders will multiply as the model spreads out to individual schools. As LEAs are weakened so that they cannot authoritatively monitor what is going on in schools' contracting activities, there are virtually no checks on how contract relations will be managed between highly skilled corporate lobbyists and voluntary governing bodies.

At the heart of the problem is the fact that these new education markets are being fashioned by government in response to firms' requests that they be created. It is not the case that an unsatisfied demand exists to which firms are responding; the demand is shaped to suit what the suppliers want to do, not what consumers want to receive. We must again remember that it is government, not the citizen-consumer, who is the customer in the commercialised welfare state.

Conclusions: Democracy, authority, citizenship

If a service is an attribute of citizenship, it is managed through concepts of rights, participation and democratic authority. Fundamental to the historical operation of the British education system was the role of elected councillors wielding political authority; LEAs administered an area's schools under the formal authority of councillors. Parents could in principle make representations to councillors about the quality of services or problems they had with their children's schools; and LEA staff were able to take firm action on such issues as individual schools' admissions practices because they acted as public authorities.

In practice the system did not always work like that; unless parents knew how to exercise pressure, the local political system could easily slip into lethargy, and this may have been particularly likely to occur in one-party dominated areas with low educational expectations – a situation that characterised many Labour towns and cities. And unless there was dynamic professional leadership, LEA staff could also be inactive. But these weaknesses are open to reform; the mechanisms exist, they only want energetic stimulation. The mechanisms themselves have to be stripped away as the public education service is redefined to become a commercial service like any other. So long as the special citizenship characteristics are recognised, commercial firms are at a disadvantage in rivalling LEAs as providers. This is especially the case when virtually all the staff deployed by the private firms are former LEA staff; all that distinguishes them from their colleagues remaining in the public sector is that they lack the latter's public authority. If however most of the special attributes of public service are defined away and its activities translated into commercial terms, the balance shifts radically the other way; being outside the public sector is, by a trick of definition, changed from being a disadvantage to an advantage.

Because the actual delivery of education in schools was until recently seen as the core business, initial commercialisation was concentrated on authority functions. This was paradoxical, as the normal situation is for privatised industries to be monitored by public regulatory authorities. In education it has been the other way round. When Ofsted was established in 1994, it differed from the existing HM Inspectorate of Schools in contracting out rather than maintaining its own staff. Initially over 80 per cent of inspection teams were provided by the staff of LEA advisory and inspection services. However, many individuals discovered that they could earn more money by setting up inspection consultancies. Today, about 75 per cent of school inspections are contracted out to private firms, in an 'industry' which was already worth around £118 million in 1997.[20]

When a private firm is invited to take over an LEA's functions because the authority is deemed to have 'failed', the administration of education in that area ceases to be a matter for local democracy, and does not even become one for local consumers. Instead it becomes a contractual relationship between central government and a privileged provider. Even when services for a 'failing' authority are provided by another LEA, the principle of local democratic accountability is broken. Within the 'failed' area the new authority providing the services has the same status as a private contractor; it does the work as part of a market contract, not as an element of local democracy.

When an LEA enters a commercialisation arrangement voluntarily, the situation might seem different: the private firms are merely contractors, agents subject to the will of their principal, which remains the legally constituted local political authority. But the political context is one in which, as we have seen, central government clearly favours the agents over the principals. Further, the fact that the LEA staff on whom the political authority depends for information and advice have been put into the position of competitors with rather than watch-dogs over contractors, combined with the long-term nature of the contracts, make difficult any effective control of agent by principal. The system is too new for us to judge how extensively chains of sub-contracting will develop, but if they do the current situation on the privatised railways demonstrates clearly how attempts by public authorities to regulate become caught in the labyrinth of contract law and inter-firm deals.

Now, the Government rarely speaks of commercial firms alone. LEAs are also invited to consider hiving off their services to religious organisations, voluntary sector partners, or even to other LEAs who may be able to offer a more efficient service.[21] Schools, like hospitals, have increasingly come to depend on volunteer help to overcome the staff shortages caused by their inadequate budgets of the 1980s and 1990s. However, commercial firms have far stronger incentives to push their role and win contracts than do voluntary organisations, especially as the efforts which a firm makes to win a contract can be offset against taxation as an acceptable business expense. Far from encouraging a growth in the role of the voluntary sector, commercialisation is likely to drive out its existing contribution. This has already happened in the case of careers advice services privatised during the 1980s by the Conservatives. At first charitable organisations bid for and won some of the contracts to replace the public service here. Gradually most have dropped away, being replaced by profit-making firms.

The provision of services by one LEA to the population of another raises different issues. A providing LEA cannot act as a democratically responsible local authority in the territory of another. As the Government's provisions make clear, within that territory the new LEA takes the form of a company, operating a commercial contract; similarly when a school takes over a poorly performing neighbour. This becomes another way of redefining the public authority role of local government as no different from commercial activity. The same is true for voluntary bodies; they take on the legal form of private contractors if they take on public education contracts. Another example is Connexions, the body established in 2001 to take over all supervision of the national careers advice service for young people, and various special services to young people with certain problems. Its local branches, which provide services for groups of local authority areas, are established as limited liability companies rather than as normal public-service organisations. The local units already remarkably incorporate named private firms into their formal governance structure. As this model grows, the normal mode of delivering local education services becomes that of the privileged insider commercial firm; the firm becomes the only acceptable form of organisation; and public service becomes an anomaly within its own heartland.

3| Towards a redefinition of public service

Challenging the hegemony of the ideology of commercialisation will not be easy. As the previous chapters have shown, this is not a problem of passing fashion or venal politicians. Extremely powerful economic forces have gathered around the project of bringing potentially lucrative citizenship services fully into the market place. In doing so they are first stripping these services of those qualities which have been part of their special value but which cannot be squeezed into the market mould. The final stage will be the presentation of these services like any other good in the market to individual consumers, so that their egalitarian, redistributive and shared character becomes entirely lost. Once this has happened, the democratisation of citizenship and the achievement of a state which worked for all people and not just privileged elites, the great achievement of the second half of the 20th century, will have been reversed.

The fight back against these threats has to present an alternative reform agenda. While the caricature of British health and education services being presented by New Labour and Conservatives alike as some kind of rigidified centralised bureaucracy of uncaring incompetents is inaccurate, it is important to recognise weaknesses which appeared in their structure and practice and which require addressing if a new public service model is to be constructed.

Redefining public service professionalism

One of the subtlest of the conflicts over the commercialisation wave of the past two decades has been that over professional knowledge, and it is here that the key will be found to a genuine third way, a true alternative to both bureaucratic centralism and commercialisation. Two kinds of such knowledge are involved. First is the professionalism of public administration itself; second is the professionalism of the knowledge-based activities delivered by the services – primarily medicine and teaching, but extending more generally to other social-service occupations, and not just the professions as conventionally understood.

The former returns us to the Victorian concept that a healthy competitive capitalism required a state that maintained the rules that regulated the market system, and was neutral in its relations to individual business interests. This model was ideal for transformation into the administration demanded by the social democratic welfare state: not in the pockets of business lobbies, and dedicated to the delivery of impartial and therefore universal and reasonably egalitarian services. However, these very qualities meant a public service that was aloof, remote, not adept at communication. It was elitist, as its professional competence rested on the assumption that a central administrative class could determine the needs of the public without much interaction other than that provided by the formal parliamentary process. Much of the unfeeling centralism of public service which Blair and his colleagues blame entirely on the post-war Labour Governments is really a residue of a pre-democratic, monarchical state with which social democracy compromised and turned to its purposes. To see what a social democratic public service is like one should look, not to the UK but to Scandinavia, where social democratic governments had far longer to develop the concept than the few years of Labour government that the UK had before the 1980s. While the Swedish and other Nordic states certainly embodied elitist and centralising ideas, they gradually developed habits of openness and transparency considerably exceeding anything found in the UK even today. They also developed models of decentralised provision and consumer choice within the framework of public service as far back as the 1970s. It is the weakness of social democratic influence on traditional models of public service that has retarded sensitivity to citizens' needs in the British case, not the dominance of social democracy over the market. It is therefore possible to seek solutions to problems of remoteness and lack of choice within the terms of the social democratic model.

There has in fact been no frontal assault on the centralised character of British public service during New Labour's reforms, partly because, as noted in the first chapter, the commercialising and privatising state needs a centralised administration, though ministers adversely compare an alleged lack of responsiveness to public concerns of public service with an idealised image of a customer-friendly private sector. When services are contracted out by a public authority to private firms, the 'customer' is not the consumer but the public authority concerned. Any improved service to ultimate consumers provided by private contractors occurs because their government customer stipulates that it wants such an improvement. If citizens play a part in formulating that stipulation it is through the political process, not the market; government becomes aware that the voters want more responsive services, and in theory demands that its private service suppliers provide them. But if government can respond to that pressure by seeking consumer-responsiveness from private firms, it could if it so chose do the same – only more directly – by stipulating better service from public providers.

Public administration and public services must become more participative and consultative. We already have the rudiments of such an approach; government needs only to turn its attention to enhancing these: for example, the practice, started by the Labour Governments of the 1970s, but sustained in diluted form since, of public participation exercises for local planning issues. Closely related were the same Governments' Community Health Councils, Conservative Governments' extensions of the participative scope and powers of school governing bodies and the current New Deal for Communities initiative. These and similar ventures could be considerably strengthened in power and deepened in scope. It is often objected that vociferous middle-class groups take more than their share of attention at such forums. That argument makes a case for community-level work to raise the participative potential of other groups and classes, not for moving back to non-participative centralism.

Also, however, one of the main desired outcomes of a consultative approach to administration and service delivery is the effect it has on the ways in which public officials and professionals tackle their tasks and engage in dialogue with the public. As they gradually learn to deal with public challenge and demands for openness, they develop ways of working which can take such challenges in their stride rather than treat them as threats. Even if they acquire these skills initially in relations with only some social groups, the change in style gradually spreads to become a new professional norm. From there it can be transferred to become an essential part of professional training and qualification.

There is considerable potential in this path. But before examining it further we must examine the other characteristic of many public services which is a strength in need of renewal, but which can clash with the demand for openness and consultation: the knowledge base on which professionalism rests. This has not figured prominently in recent conflict over services. While ministers and private contractors caricature many characteristics of those who work in public service, it is more difficult to ridicule their knowledge. Most voters would feel uneasy if ministers and managing directors without professional training decided that they could tell surgeons how to perform operations or teachers how to educate.

But a covert attack on knowledge has been taking place. Notoriously the internal market system imposed on the NHS by the Conservative Government did involve medically unqualified managers challenging clinical judgement, as methods of work measurement imitated from the management of low-skilled factory work were imposed on medical practice as part of cost-cutting drives. Strangely, given the generally superior professional status claimed by medical practitioners against school teachers, education has managed to sustain the model of administration by persons experienced within the profession more effectively. Further, as we saw in the previous chapter, so far the private firms moving into education are depending very heavily on recruiting both administrative and teaching staff from those trained for the public profession. The undermining of existing structures of schools and LEAs takes the form mainly of allegations that those practising the profession are not worthy of its ideals. Indeed, the establishment by the Government of the General Teaching Council, modelled even in its name as an analogy of the General Medical Council, has been an enormous boost to the concept of the teaching profession, as well as constituting an element of the New Labour approach on which a further reconstruction of the profession could constructively build.

Also useful is the fact that the insertion of strictly commercial, profit-making structures into British education is an oddity even in the private sector. The elite parts of the historical private sector of schools have always had charitable status; only a questionable fringe has taken pure commercial form. Whatever one thinks about the entitlement of fee-paying schools to be regarded as 'charities', this fact does indicate deeply held beliefs that there is something anomalous about seeking to mix the profession with pure commercialism.

Disquiet at commercialisation and continuing recognition of the distinction between activities for profit and not for profit strongly suggest that a defence of public services based on respect for their knowledge is entirely feasible. There are however two major obstacles to advance on this front: first, much of the agenda for public service reform requires the undermining of professional responsibility. Second, although successive governments can be fairly blamed for destroying professional morale, the professions should not automatically be trusted to develop an appropriate new approach provided only that government would leave them alone. These problems merit close consideration.

The problem of government undermining

The Government has recently realised that the constant attacks of itself and its Conservative predecessors against the public service professions has had negative effects, not only on recruitment to the occupations concerned, but also by creating a mood of cynicism, which naturally reduced commitment to reform. As the Government's education adviser, Michael Barber, has neatly expressed the point, since the 1970s education services had moved from a position of guidance by uninformed professional judgement, through one of uninformed national prescription during the 1980s, to one of informed national prescription during the 1990s.[22] What was needed for the new century was a pattern of informed professional judgement replacing the national prescription. In similar spirit, the Prime Minister has spoken in his Fabian pamphlet, *The Courage of Our Convictions,* of the need for high-quality, high-morale services.[23] As he made clear, the Government also sees that loosening the grip of central bureaucracy on the professions is fundamental to improving their morale. But the same pamphlet also demonstrates the dichotomous way in which he regards this issue: centralisation and neglect of the consumer is the product of the post-war Old Labour model of uniform public services; and decentralised customer friendliness is an essential attribute of private firms. This enables ministers to present the introduction of private contractors as an automatic resolution of the problems of neglect of 'customers', and to ignore the contribution to centralisation and low morale being made by the proliferation of central imposed targets and evaluations that is fundamental to their own Government's approach.

As Onora O'Neill has remarked, while targets are justified by a declared need to restore 'trust' in the public service professions, they do not seem to have any such effect; because, in general, politicians are less trusted than are the professions.[24] A shift in the system of guaranteeing the quality of services from professions to politicians is a shift to a system less worthy of trust. She also shows how Government places contradictory targets on public services, enabling itself to claim that it is pursuing all the goals, while pushing resolution of the problem on to the practitioners. In fact, it does this in its approach to the problem of reconstituting professionalism itself. At one level ministers declare their commitment to the professions and to the ethic of public service, while at another they intensify further the targeting strategy and the commercialisation which undermine these same things.

A new reform strategy for public service must include a changed approach to assessment and measurement of actual performance, away from the stock exchange model of indicatorism and towards professionalism. Performance assessment by professionals aims at whole service appraisal, using qualified expert judgement to take account of how practitioners have balanced conflicting goals. It is also capable of assessing fine points and nuances and not just global targets. It certainly makes use of check lists and explicit lists of criteria of judgement, and will use quantitative measures where these derive directly and clearly from the activity concerned, but it is not entirely dependent on these. It was the kind of model that used to be followed by HM Inspectorate of Schools (HMI), and is in fact still practised by that Inspectorate in its residual but important role. While evaluation reports of this kind are serious technical documents, it is also possible to produce reduced versions of, say, reports on individual schools or hospital departments which are accessible and comprehensible to a wider public. They probably do not lend themselves easily to use in constructing league tables, but given the crudity and vulnerability to manipulation and misuse of that approach, this is no bad thing.

The problem with the HMI approach to evaluation is that it is expensive, as it requires a large number of highly skilled professionals capable of assessing the work of their peers. The impact of HMI was gradually weakened over decades as governments cut back on it; schools would be inspected too rarely for follow-up and evaluation of measures taken to address weaknesses to be effective. The current system of appraisal by numerical indicators dispenses with the need for a high quality of inspectors. This has been particularly helpful to the privatisation process. Private firms bid competitively for school inspection work because they can employ for relatively low fees retired education personnel, including of course those who have been quietly 'pensioned off' because of unsatisfactory performance as teachers.

But great gains would compensate for the cost of high-skilled inspection, as professionals were encouraged to turn their attention away from playing with targets. They would see the professional model of working substantively and not just rhetorically supported by government. And they would see an approach to achieving high standards that emerges sui generis from the specific characteristics of the public service professions themselves, not off-the-shelf borrowing of inappropriate business analogies. This would be the right starting point for a rediscovery of the concept of high professional standards, instilled initially in training and sustained subsequently by truly professional monitoring, inspecting and, where necessary, disciplining.

The problem of professional arrogance

If head teachers, senior LEA staff, and teachers' trade unions and professional associations are firm in their insistence on high-quality performance, those seeking to undermine the system will have little justification for external intervention. If they are slack and indulgent of weakness and poor performance, they destroy the principal ground on which they stand. This is a responsibility which every individual working in the system can assume for themselves, but a special burden rests with the wide range of relevant associations and unions. It is not in the interests of teachers in general if their representative bodies protect poor-quality practice or seek to reduce pressures for high performance. If we reject attempts to improve quality by payment-by-results schemes, there is an obligation to develop other, truly professional means of quality improvement.

Those involved in managing professional associations and training programmes must avoid an opposition-mindedness that means they reject all government policies for improvement just because they emanate from government. It must be fully recognised that many initiatives by successive governments of the past 20 years have contributed to a better education service: establishment of a National Curriculum, more intensive inspectorial work, the assertion of high standards of teaching and educational performance as a major national concern.

We need professions that are open, committed to dialogue and public participation, but proud of their special knowledge. There are clear tensions here. Can these really be reconciled? The more that a profession insists on its integrity and capacity for self-discipline, the more it is likely to protect its mystique. Conservative members of the professions would probably claim that much of their recent trouble results from their increased openness in recent years, their willingness to accept political, media and public scrutiny. The temptation to resolve this dilemma by running in either direction is strong. In one direction one pulls up the drawbridge again and reasserts the inscrutable character of the profession's knowledge, warding off all who seek to pry. The alternative extreme response is to try to duck below the parapet: to drop all claims to being anything special, to deny that the activity has any knowledge of particular importance. This was how many in teaching, at all levels – but never medicine – responded to the first stress of demands for scrutiny and openness in the 1970s. It was accompanied by the challenge of comprehensive education, which for the first time raised public and political expectations for the educational achievements of all children. Today, in a period when New Labour is toying with ways of restoring selective education, it is hard to recall how, while the old 11 plus system dominated, there was little concern for the educational performance of the bottom 65-70 per cent of the age range who went to secondary modern schools, few of whom took any measurable performance tests for the rest of their school careers. Or rather, all concern that was expressed took the form of the campaign to end selection. Obviously, mere change of the system did not solve the problems of educating all these children in a different way. There was considerable uncertainty, and many members of the teaching profession – which had in any case expanded massively, often with inadequate training – responded to the challenges and the new level of public concern by scaling down the claims that could be made for the educational process. Curricula became undemanding, and while teachers were often right to make education child-centred in the sense of meeting the children where they were, they often then simply stayed there, doing little to create challenging aspirations. Far from insisting on its mystique, teaching seemed to want to deconstruct itself. The political reaction against this continues today.

The dilemma between an open and consultative approach on one hand and the cultivation of a high level of professionalism on the other seems difficult, but running in either direction at the expense of the other will be disastrous. Fortunately, this is one of those rare issues where, with imagination and willingness to adjust, the best of both worlds can be had: an assured and confident insistence on professional competence can combine with a willingness to share special knowledge with clients, the general public and the political world. This is achieved surprisingly frequently. For example, many a primary school head teacher has learned how to talk openly and in detail about her work to meetings of governors and of parents without feeling that this compromises her possession of special knowledge and understanding, but also without needing to pretend that her knowledge and understanding are worthless. To take a different profession, medical practitioners are today likely to be willing to tell a patient that he has a terminal cancer, and to discuss openly with him the prognosis and helpful measures that they will take together to make things easier. In earlier times they hid behind a wall of professional secrecy which served to spare them the need to engage in painful dialogue with a fellow human being.

If earlier generations of professional practitioners hid behind their mystique, it was partly because their knowledge base did not live up to their claims. Until the late 19th century medicine really had little to offer many of its patients. Teachers until an even later date were largely ignorant of the psychology and sociology of the education process. Their early 21st century successors have no need for such defensiveness. Their knowledge base and set of competences will not be laid waste in the course of frank and open-hearted exchanges with clients, or discussions in parent-teacher and doctor-patient committees.

The revival of local government

Historically Labour has been the most consistently centralising party in the British state, through all its shifts between right and left. It used to identify local government with entrenched squirearchies and urban bourgeois elites, and worried that local power meant an inability to redistribute resources from richer to poorer geographical areas. During the long years of the highly centralist Thatcher Government it really seemed that Labour, reduced to its urban strongholds, had discovered the political value of local government. This was one of the few things that united the urban left, struggling against deindustrialisation and the dismantling of the welfare state, with New Labour, seeking new radical themes that would cut associations with the state-centralising tendencies of the old Labour Party.[25] Devolution to Scotland, Wales and Northern Ireland, enhanced English regionalism, and anti-centralising constitutional reforms were fundamental to the 1997 package. In reality, once the formal commitments to the Celtic nations had been honoured, New Labour showed itself to be as centralising as either Thatcherism or Bevanism. In the Introduction we examined reasons why this has been a paradoxical part of the commercialisation agenda itself.

There are virtuous or vicious spirals at work here. In the virtuous spiral, local levels of government assert strength and achieve high standards because they can attract both politicians and professional staff of high calibre, and be equipped with the resources they need to provide a high-class service. They can attract such staff because a sympathetic central government is willing to engage in a major and serious decentralisation of competences and control over resources to prominent, well established multi-purpose authorities. In such a way, bringing the administration of many elements of the health service within general local government would both increase its democratic accountability and enhance the status of local government. For too long the UK has been in precisely the reverse, vicious spiral, as stripping local government of powers has reinforced and been reinforced by a decline in the quality of its personnel. The needs of the commercialisation agenda for even more centralisation are adding further, eventually fatal, twists to the vicious spiral.

In persuading government to shift to the virtuous spiral, one can point to positive aspects of recent developments in bench-marking, auditing and the targeting of achievements. Although much has been said above about the negative consequences of excessive targeting, a more restrained and finely judged use of these devices can make possible a model of maximum decentral-isation accompanied by truly professional evaluation and inspec-tion to ensure that standards are maintained and a stable, limited number of major central policy goals met. The local and national prominence given today to such things as the inspection of local education authorities and schools' achievements do at least show that there can be a lively local democracy around movements for improved standards. At present these devices have been accom-panied by rather than substituted for increasing centralised control. More logical and positively challenging to morale and competence would be a high level of scrutiny accompanying radically increased autonomy – and the autonomy needs to be professional and concerned with actual service delivery, not just the ambiguous autonomy of financial responsibility. Such autonomy should indeed include the right to contract out non-core services if authorities so wish – provided one could have confidence that central government and its monitoring agencies would be willing to take a neutral view of the performance of such services.

Recommendations

From the above discussion flow a number of practical proposals for a strategy of modernising public services in a manner which is compatible with the concept of the welfare state as a fundamental component of social citizenship. To the extent that the 'problem' of the welfare state is seen as one of the quality of services provided to citizens, there is no reason why these proposals should not be acceptable within a New Labour agenda. It is only if the main concerns of that agenda are a determination to provide new profitable areas for private firms ahead of improving services to citizens, or to shift the burden of costs of public services from collective provision to the individual user, that there is any incompatibility with these proposals.

First come a number of measures which are needed to clarify the role of both citizenship and the market (as well as other forms of commercialisation) within the public services. The measures are needed, not just to protect citizenship rights from being undermined by commercialisation, but to protect the market from corruption in this unavoidably politicised arena.

■ While there is certainly a role for private suppliers of marginal and ancillary aspects of public services, extreme care must be taken about such involvement in the core business of citizenship services, since removing core business from the realm of citizenship and placing it within the market constitutes a major derogation of citizenship entitle-

71

ment. Avoidance of distortion and residualisation must be regarded as part of the definition of high standards and efficiency in the delivery of services. The next step of policy development must be to debate and then to define the citizenship core, which must then be ring-fenced from commercialisation.

■ The importance of direct political access by citizens to issues of service quality must be strengthened in services considered essential to citizenship rights. Achieving this goal will mean maximal devolution to lower levels of government for service delivery and minimal contracting out to private suppliers. Since commercialisation gives true customer status only to government as the principal in contracting out, it is not a response to problems of remoteness from citizens. Far more logical would be determined attempts to improve the citizenship quality of public services through measures for increased decentralisation and participation.

■ Lobbying by private firms for the award of contracts to run public services in the non-core areas where they should be expected to remain active, must be subject to strict, independent and open scrutiny. If there are to be markets, they must be as close as possible to true markets, and not those corrupted by clientelistic links and cronyism. This requires the establishment of new monitoring procedures at both central and local government levels. The only way to ensure high standards is to make it illegal for any firm which makes donations of a political nature, or seconds staff to ministries or think tanks, to be allowed to bid for public contracts. Furthermore, in the interests of providing a level playing field among competing firms and avoiding insider lobbying, all policy planning concerning the entry of private firms into public service contracts should be carried out in consultation with associations representing the firms in the relevant sector, not with individual enterprises.

Next comes the need to restructure the place of the public service professions. As with the relationship between citizenship and the market, the needs here are two-edged. The morale of these professions has been desperately undermined by attacks by successive governments on the public services and their funding, as well as by government determination to bring in commercial criteria. At the same time, however, some traditional approaches of the professions to their clients need to be changed if the aims of citizenship services are genuinely to be realised.

- There must be a revitalisation of the concept of professional responsibility within public service, extending through the knowledge-based services, administration itself, and all other occupations involved in public-service delivery. Government at all levels, professional institutions, and those responsible for training and management share an obligation to work on this.

- New concepts of professional knowledge and skill must include capacity for open communication and dialogue with service users and citizens in general as fundamental components. These principles must be fundamentally embedded in training, management and evaluation activities.

- Reinvigorated professional models of evaluating service performance and dealing with poor performance must replace excessive and overly politicised reliance on benchmarking and targeting. But monitoring and auditing of performance remain fundamental.

Confident, communicative openness based on constantly improving skills, alongside centrally monitored local democracy, must be the hallmarks of a new public service. These needs extend to the profession of administration itself, which must learn to regard a capacity to engage in public consultation and participation as part of its skill, rather than as an occasional nightmare to be avoided as much as possible. Training programmes and management systems for all groups who deliver citizenship services need to instil and enforce capacity for and pride in both expertise and two-way communication. These attributes can be pitted against the greater need for secrecy that will always characterise the commercial sector because of firms' needs to protect their business practices from imitation by competitors. The more that the model of open, consultative, authoritatively monitored professionalism in public services is a reality in the lives of citizens, the more likely it is that the citizenship welfare state, far from creeping from the historical stage, may yet experience its finest hours.

Crouch, C. 1999, Social Change in Western Europe. Oxford: Oxford University Press.

References

1. Series of articles on the Private Finance Initiative in the NHS, A Pollock et al, *British Medical Journal*, 1999

2. *Social Change in Western Europe*, C Crouch, Oxford Univeristy Press, 1999

3. *Sociology at the Crossroads and Other Essays*, T H Marshall, RKP, 1963

4. *Exit, Voice, and Loyalty: Responses to Decline in Firms, Organizations, and States* A Hirschman, Harvard University Press, 2001

5. *The Gift Relationship: from Human Blood to Social Policy*, R M Titmuss, Allen & Unwin, 1970

6. 'The Marketization of Public Services' by M R Freedland, *Citizenship, Markets and the State*, C Crouch, K Eder and D Tambini (ed), Clarendon Press, 2001

7. *No Logo: No Space, No Choice, No Jobs, Taking Aim at the Brand Bullies*, N Klein, Flamingo, 2000

8. 'Where the Third Way goes from Here: renewing progressive politics' by Tony Blair in *Progressive Politics*, 2003

9. 'Called to Account', O O'Neill, Lecture no 3 in 'A Question of Trust', the BBC Reith Lectures, 2002.

10. 'Against Privatizing Schools in the UK' by H Brighouse, *London Review of Education*, 2003

11. 'The Price of Funny Money' by L Dalton in *What's It All About?*, Secondary Heads Association, 2002

12 *Times Educational Supplement* 19 November 1999

13. 'The Changing Role of the LEA', Department for Education and Skills, 2001

14. *ibid.*

15. Learning and Skills Act, 2000

16. *Times Educational Supplement* 19 November 1999

17. 'Schools under New Labour – Getting down to Business' Paper

presented by R Hatcher at 'Privatisierung des Bildungsbereichs', University of Hamburg.

18. *Times Educational Supplement* 13 July 2001

19. *Times Educational Supplement* 25 May 2001

20. *Times Educational Supplement* 19 December 1997

21. Letter from Secretary of State to CEOs explaining her new 'brokerage' concept of LEAs, 6 July 2001

22. 'Large-Scale Education Reform in England: A Work in Progress' by M Barber, School Development Conference, Tart University, Estonia, 2001

23. *The Courage of Our Convictions*, T Blair, Fabian Society, 2002

24. 'Called to Account', O O'Neill, Lecture no 3 in 'A Question of Trust', the BBC Reith Lectures, 2002.

25. *European Cities: Social Conflicts and Governance*, P Le Galès, Oxford University Press, 2002

Other Fabian Society Publications

Coping with Post-democracy

Colin Crouch

'In this stimulating pamphlet, Professor Colin Crouch makes links between the decline of the state and the waning of democratic enthusiasm. When so much of the public sector has been handed over to private operators, Crouch argues, what becomes of the image of government as a task that matters? If every public function is tested by its conformity with private-sector management goals, why should anyone get excited about choosing between parties? If government is routInely seen as incompetent, and the company as the only source of expertise, no wonder politics and democracy, in America if not yet here, are at an all-time low. This is a fate that Labour, not so long ago, would have been desperate to avoid. At some stage, the Labour Party may have to confront the lacuna that has been created on the left.'
Hugo Young, The *Guardian*

Colin Crouch is Professor of Sociology at the European University Institute, Florence, and External Scientific member of the Max Planck Institute for Society Research, Cologne

December 2000 ISBN 07163 0598 4 £6.95

Email bookshop@fabian-society.org.uk or call 020 7227 4900

The Courage of Our Convictions
Why reform of the public services is the route to social justice

Tony Blair

In this Fabian pamphlet the Prime Minster sets out the arguments for public service reform and warns that unless this is done successfully tax-funded public services could be lost altogether.

Tony Blair argues that public services are crucial to Labour's goal of social justice. Acknowledging that tension exists between national audits and inspections and local autonomy, Blair argues that this can be overcome and sets out his four principles of reform: national standards, devolved power, professionalism and choice.

December 2002 ISBN 07163 0603 4 £6.95

Email bookshop@fabian-society.org.uk or call 020 7227 4900

Paying for Progress
A New Politics of Tax for Public Spending

The Commission on Taxation and Citizenship

Taxation—and the public spending it pays for—is the subject of the fiercest political controversy. *Paying for Progress: A New Politics of Tax for Public Spending* offers a compelling new approach.

Reporting new research into public attitudes towards taxation, Paying for Progress argues that the public must be 'reconnected' to the taxes they pay and the public services which these finance. To do this it proposes the greater use of 'earmarked' taxes, including a new tax to fund the National Health Service. Setting out a new philosophy of citzenship to underpin taxation policy, it recommends a series of reforms to meet the goals of social inclusion and environmental protection.

Written in a lively and accessible style, *Paying for Progress* makes an important contribution to political thought and policy in the first decade of the 21st century. Providing key information on the UK tax system, it will also be an invaluable text for students and researchers in politics, economics, public administration, law and accountancy.

'Coherent, radical and lucid... this important book raises critical questions for the future of British politics'
Will Hutton, Chief Executive, the Industrial Society

'The clarity with which it explores the facts and arguments about the tax system make it an extremely valuable text for students and researchers. It will provide a benchmark for future work on taxation reform'
Andrew Gamble, Professor of Politics, University of Sheffield

November 2000 ISBN 07163 6003 9 £9.95

Email bookshop@fabian-society.org.uk or call 020 7227 4900

FABIAN SOCIETY

Get ahead of Labour's thinking — join the Fabian Society now for just £8.95

Members receive:

- 3 issues of our highly regarded magazine, *Fabian Review*

- 2 pamphlets on key political and policy ideas

- Advance notice of our headline political conferences

- Access to a nationwide network of over 70 local Fabian groups

'The Fabians perform the vital function of thinking beyond the current news agenda – and beyond current government orthodoxy. Whether it's on tax, public services, globalisation or the environment, they are never afraid to ask difficult questions.'
Polly Toynbee, The *Guardian*

'I am constantly impressed by the quality of the Fabians' conferences and meetings. The Society provides a unique forum for real people to debate real ideas – the lifeblood of a political movement.'
Will Hutton, The Work Foundation

'The Fabians provide a vital space for debate between pressure groups and their members, the wider public, and political parties and government. It's a critical role for democracy.'
Stephen Tindale, Greenpeace UK

For a membership form please ring 020 7227 4900 or email info@fabian-society.org.uk